EVERYTHING
PREDATORS

EVERYTHING PREDATORS

Blake Hoena
With National Geographic Explorer Shivani Bhalla

CONTENTS

Green tree pythons live in or near rain forests, where they are known to rest coiled around tree branches, or in bushes.

Cheetahs are the fastest land animals.

INTRODUCTION

DANGEROUS AND DEADLY.
THAT'S HOW WE THINK OF PREDATORS SUCH

as big cats, bears, and wolves. But predators are so much more. Many predators, such as the polar bear, are incredibly strong and famously formidable. Others, such as the king cobra, are stealthy, fast, and venomous. They can be as large as a sperm whale or as small as a jumping spider. Predators are many things, including a vital part of many food chains and food webs.

Many animals are considered predators—probably more than you ever imagined. It's surprising how varied predators are. We are all familiar with mighty hunters such as lions, tigers, eagles, and sharks. They are top predators, with jaws, teeth, and sharp claws for tearing flesh. But what about panfish, fireflies, sea stars, and hedgehogs? You might not think of these unassuming creatures as predators. But they are! The natural world is full of animals that need to eat, and many catch and eat other animals. So read on to learn EVERYTHING about the amazingly diverse world of predators.

EXPLORER'S CORNER

Hi! I'm Shivani Bhalla.

I'm from Kenya, where I was lucky enough to go on wildlife safaris as a child. These safaris helped me develop a passion for big cats. I saw my first cheetah when I was only eight years old, and I never forgot that moment. That was when I decided I wanted to be a wildlife conservationist so I could protect these animals. Through my passion for cats and conservation, I started the Ewaso Lions Project, based in Samburu, northern Kenya. The project helps people and big cats live in the same environment. Throughout this book in these Explorer's Corners, I will share with you stories about my life and work. Can you guess what animals I am taking pictures of here in my photo? Clue: Look closely. They are endangered predators. Check for the answer on page 36.

1

AT FIRST BITE

Steller's sea eagles are large and strong birds that prey on salmon and other fish. They breed and nest along the coast of eastern Russia.

WHAT IS A PREDATOR?

THE SIMPLE ANSWER IS THAT

A PREDATOR IS ANY ANIMAL THAT HUNTS AND eats other animals. In the wild, hunger and the need to survive drive a predator's killer instincts.

POWER IN NUMBERS

Predators are typically larger than their prey. Think of a gecko snacking on an insect or a fox chasing down a rabbit. But size doesn't always matter. Wolves hunt together, and a pack's combined strength can take down a moose or a Bactrian camel—animals many times the size of a lone wolf. Lions, dolphins, baboons, and ants are also known to hunt together. Numbers help to overwhelm large prey. But hunting together has other advantages, too. Predators can coordinate their attack, even against smaller animals.

A pod of long-beaked common dolphins circle a school of fish. The dolphins gather together in superpods that can number in the thousands, and they break off into smaller groups that hunt and feed together.

FACT BITES: VULTURES ARE SCAVENGER BIRDS THAT FEED ON CARRION IN GROUPS.

HYENAS

AN EAS(IER) MEAL

Snakes, big cats, and many canids, or animals in the dog family such as wolves and foxes, prefer their meat fresh. Not all predators are so choosy. Some will wait for leftovers. For example, hyenas will pick over the carcass of a lion's kill. A bald eagle is just as likely to eat a dead fish washed up on shore as it is to catch a live one. And some animals, such as maggots, or fly larvae, eat a strict diet of carrion. Why eat dead animal flesh? Hunting takes a lot of energy, and not every hunt is successful. Each failed attempt means wasted energy and a growing hunger for the predator. Carrion doesn't flee or fight back, so it makes for an easier meal. Scavengers, such as raccoons, worms, crabs, and vultures, also work as nature's garbage collectors by eating carrion. In nature, very few things ever go to waste.

DINNER IS SERVED

When you think of predators, you probably think of carnivores, as in meat-eaters. Sharks, crocodiles, and hawks are a few animals that have strict diets of animal flesh. But the majority of predators are less picky. They are omnivores, eating both meat and plants, which gives them more options. Turtles are one example of an omnivorous predator. They chomp on insects, worms, and fish, but they also chow down on water lettuce and other plants. And what about those beautiful songbirds tweeting in your backyard? Most of them are omnivorous predators, too. Songbirds snatch up insects as they dart through the air, but many also eat seeds and fruits, especially when they are offered in a backyard feeder.

A Eurasian hoopoe brings an insect back to its nest. Hoopoes use their long bills to clamp onto insects.

LICE

I VANT TO SUCK YOUR BLOOD

What do you call a predator that just eats a bit of you? A micro-predator! Most predators kill their prey, and most, but not all, are larger than their prey. Micro-predators do not kill their prey, and they are smaller than their prey. Vampire bats and mosquitoes are examples of micro-predators. They feed on the blood of animals but leave them alive once they've eaten. Micro-predators also don't need a host to survive, the way a parasite does. Parasites, such as tapeworms and lice, feed off hosts that they also live in or on.

SOME **PLANTS** ARE **PREDATORS. PITCHER PLANTS** AND **FLYTRAPS FEAST** ON **ANIMALS. MOST EAT INSECTS, BUT** SOME ARE BIG ENOUGH TO **CAPTURE** SMALL **MICE** AND **FROGS.**

WHAT'S FOR DINNER?

EAT OR BE EATEN. THAT'S HOW NATURE WORKS, ESPECIALLY IN THE

world of predators. It's not always easy to separate the predators from the prey, however. That's because there are so many animals that eat other animals for food. And some eat each other. For instance, a rat snake may slither into a hawk's nest to eat some eggs, and even hatchlings are vulnerable prey. But adult hawks commonly feast on snakes, too.

ENERGY FROM THE SUN

Food webs and food chains show how living things get their food. Each living thing is part of a food chain. Food webs are made up of a number of connected chains. And it all starts with the sun. Mixed with rain and nutrients in the soil, the sun provides the energy plants need to grow. Plants, with their seeds and fruit, are the world's main source of food.

Some snakes eat bird eggs, but birds such as hawks also eat snakes.

ECOSYSTEMS

An ecosystem includes all living things, from plants to animals and decomposers. And there are many food chains in an ecosystem. Some living things can be a part of multiple food chains. And food chains can overlap and become food webs.

FACT BITES: HUMANS TOP OUR FOOD CHAIN, AS WE HAVE NO NATURAL PREDATORS.

WHO'S EATING WHO?

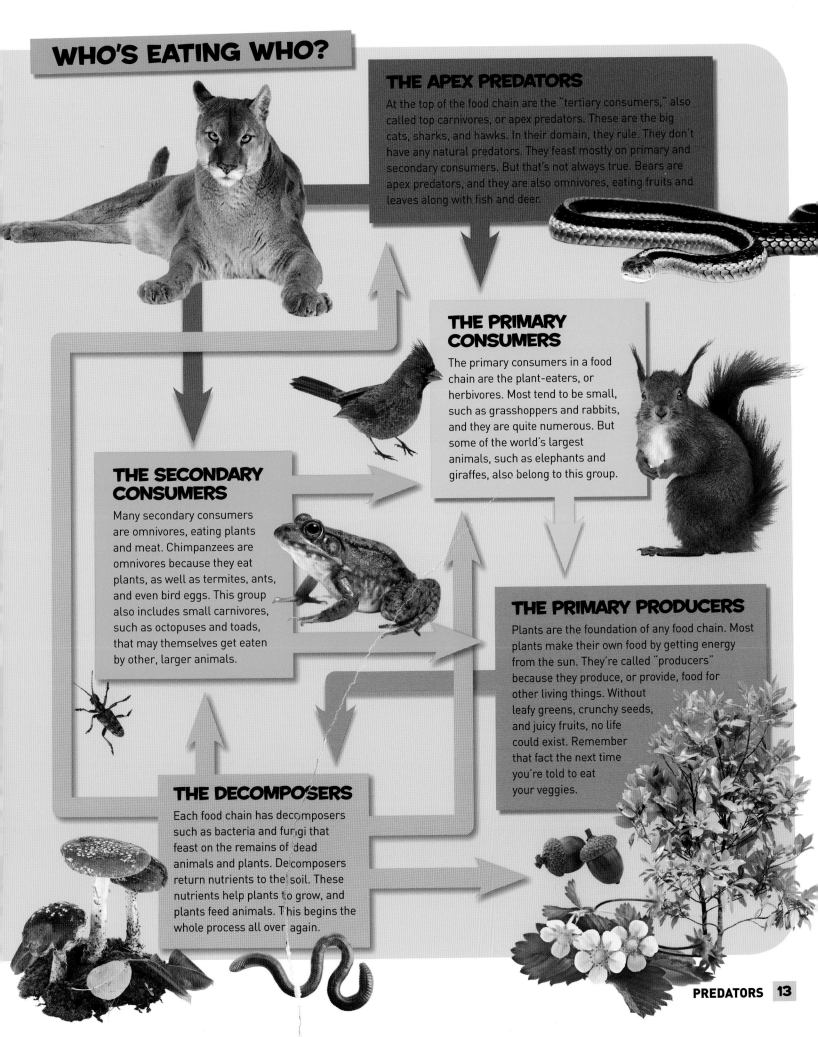

THE APEX PREDATORS

At the top of the food chain are the "tertiary consumers," also called top carnivores, or apex predators. These are the big cats, sharks, and hawks. In their domain, they rule. They don't have any natural predators. They feast mostly on primary and secondary consumers. But that's not always true. Bears are apex predators, and they are also omnivores, eating fruits and leaves along with fish and deer.

THE PRIMARY CONSUMERS

The primary consumers in a food chain are the plant-eaters, or herbivores. Most tend to be small, such as grasshoppers and rabbits, and they are quite numerous. But some of the world's largest animals, such as elephants and giraffes, also belong to this group.

THE SECONDARY CONSUMERS

Many secondary consumers are omnivores, eating plants and meat. Chimpanzees are omnivores because they eat plants, as well as termites, ants, and even bird eggs. This group also includes small carnivores, such as octopuses and toads, that may themselves get eaten by other, larger animals.

THE PRIMARY PRODUCERS

Plants are the foundation of any food chain. Most plants make their own food by getting energy from the sun. They're called "producers" because they produce, or provide, food for other living things. Without leafy greens, crunchy seeds, and juicy fruits, no life could exist. Remember that fact the next time you're told to eat your veggies.

THE DECOMPOSERS

Each food chain has decomposers such as bacteria and fungi that feast on the remains of dead animals and plants. Decomposers return nutrients to the soil. These nutrients help plants to grow, and plants feed animals. This begins the whole process all over again.

A FAMILY AFFAIR

MANY ANIMALS ARE GROUPED TOGETHER
BY SIMILAR FEATURES. FOR EXAMPLE, ALL REPTILES HAVE SOME SORT

of scaly skin, and all birds have feathers. When it comes to predators, the shared features may be pointy teeth or fangs, sharp claws or talons, and keen senses to help find, capture, and kill their prey.

PEREGRINE FALCON

BIRDS OF PREY

Many birds eat insects, fish, frogs, and other small creatures. But the best designed killers among our feathery friends are birds of prey, such as hawks, eagles, and owls. Along with their hooked beaks for tearing flesh, they have razor-sharp talons, perfect for snatching up prey. Among birds that fly, they are some of the largest, with the Andean condor having a ten-foot (3-m) wingspan. They are also some of the fastest animals on the planet, with the peregrine falcon reaching speeds of 200 miles an hour (322 km/h) while diving after prey. Another key feature common among birds of prey is that most have excellent eyesight, which allows them to soar high overhead while searching for an unsuspecting mouse scampering through a field.

FACT BITES: BLUE WHALES ARE THE WORLD'S LARGEST PREDATORS.

TOOTHY FISH

Sure, we all know sharks have pointy teeth, but they aren't the only fish to sport a deadly bite. Tigerfish and piranhas have sharp, interlocking teeth that are perfect for tearing flesh from animals. But their teeth are dull in comparison to those of a barracuda or a vampire fish, which look like rows of fangs. These fish use their long, sharp teeth for snagging prey and biting off chunks of flesh.

VAMPIRE FISH

LEOPARD

JAWS AND CLAWS

Carnivora is an order of mammals known for being, well, exactly what their name implies: carnivores. They are primarily built for eating meat. They all have strong jaws and canine teeth, which are pairs of long, sharp teeth on their top and bottom jaws. These are perfect for holding on to prey and ripping flesh from bone. They have sharp claws with at least four toes on each paw. They are also smart, and many tend to be social animals. Common animals in the group are bears, wolves, cats (including house cats), and badgers. But the group also includes weasels, skunks, seals (yes, they have claws on their flippers), and otters.

GRIZZLY BEAR

CORN SNAKE

SLITHERING SNAKES

Snakes are skilled hunters despite their lack of limbs. Many rely on patience, hiding and waiting for their prey to come to them. When it does, they strike! Once they've caught their prey, they open their flexible jaws wide to swallow animals bigger than they are wide. Snakes also have powerful muscles throughout their bodies. These muscles work somewhat like an accordion, pulling the prey down a snake's throat so slowly that it can take up to an hour to swallow a large meal. Some snakes swallow live prey, others kill or paralyze their prey with venom before eating, and some constrict their prey before swallowing it.

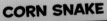

EXPLORER'S CORNER

I have lived in the wilds of Samburu for more than 13 years. This is a semi-arid desert that is very dry. But it is a great place for predators. There are many leopards, lions, and even wild dogs that roam this dry region. My work focuses on lions, where I work with local people to encourage them to tolerate and live alongside lions. Lion populations are declining across Africa. To ensure that there is a future for lions and other predators, we must work with the local people; this is key to successful conservation.

PREDATOR WORLD

WHEREVER THERE IS PREY,
THERE ARE PREDATORS. PREDATORS

are found from the Arctic, where polar bears hunt ringed seals, to Antarctica, where leopard seals snatch up penguins, and everywhere in between. Let's take a look at some unusual predators with some supercool abilities.

HUMPBACK WHALE

NORTH AMERICA

Star-Nosed Mole

With all the tentacles sticking out from its snout, this tiny mammal looks like something out of a science-fiction movie. And while it has poor eyesight, those tentacles make up for it. The touch sensors on them can detect whether something is edible, such as a beetle, or not, such as a rock.

NORTH AMERICA

STAR-NOSED MOLE

STAR-NOSED MOLE

STAR-NOSED MOLE

SOUTH AMERICA

Amazonian Giant Centipede

Arthropods can be creepy with their many legs and antennae, but imagine one that can grow up to a foot (30 cm) long! This predator is armed with up to 46 clawed feet for climbing and for grasping prey. And what's more amazing is that it can hang from the roof of a cave and catch bats mid-flight.

AMAZONIAN GIANT CENTIPEDE

SOUTH AMERICA

HUMPBACK WHALE

All predators have tricks to catch their food, but humpback whales do it with style. A pod will herd fish together by swimming around them and trapping them in a wall of bubbles. Once their prey is trapped, the humpbacks gulp down huge mouthfuls of fish.

HUMPBACK WHALE

FACT BITE: THE STAR-NOSED MOLE USES BUBBLES TO SMELL UNDERWATER.

Eurasian Lynx

Don't call out "here, kitty, kitty!" to this cat. While not as big and frightening as some of its cousins, it has no problem breaking the rule about predators hunting prey smaller than itself. A Eurasian lynx will pounce on deer and wild pigs more than twice its size.

0 — 2,000 MILES

0 — 2,000 KILOMETERS

EUROPE

ASIA

EURASIAN LYNX

AFRICA

HONEY BADGER

AUSTRALIA

Mantis Shrimp

From the venomous inland taipan to saltwater crocodiles, many deadly predators call Australia home. One of the most impressive is the tiny mantis shrimp. It has two clublike front legs that can deliver a punch powerful enough to crack a crab shell.

MANTIS SHRIMP

ARCHERFISH

MANTIS SHRIMP

WHERE PREDATORS LIVE

- [ ] Amazonian Giant Centipede
- [ ] Archerfish
- [ ] Eurasian Lynx
- [ ] Honey Badger
- [ ] Humpback Whale
- [ ] Mantis Shrimp
- [ ] Star-Nosed Mole

Archerfish

This fish grows to only about 6 inches (15 cm) long, but its aim, not its size, is what's impressive. An archerfish can shoot streams of water up to 5 feet (1.5 m) to knock insects and small lizards from branches. Once the animals fall into the water, the archerfish gobbles them up.

AUSTRALIA

HUMPBACK WHALE

AFRICA/ASIA

Honey Badger

Don't let the name fool you. A honey badger isn't sweet at all. It just likes honey. What's amazing about the mammal is its strength and fearlessness. It will aggressively defend itself against lions and leopards. And it's not a picky eater. It'll eat whatever it can find, even munching on venomous snakes and scorpions.

By the Numbers

3,000 snake species are estimated to live throughout the world

450 species of birds of prey live throughout the world

400 shark species are estimated to live in the world's oceans

270 carnivora species exist on the planet

A PHOTOGRAPHIC DIAGRAM

BEAKS AND TEETH

BEAKS AND TEETH
ARE SOME OF THE TOOLS OF THE
trade for predators. After all, many predators can't kill or eat without them.

Beaks come in all shapes and sizes. Each type of beak works slightly differently to help birds and other beaked creatures catch and eat their prey.

TEARING
Birds of prey, such as owls and hawks, have sharp, hook-shaped beaks perfect for piercing, tugging skin, and tearing flesh.

STRIKING
Herons and egrets have long, pointed beaks designed for striking and snatching fish and frogs out of the water. Then, with a tilt of their head, they gulp down their prey whole.

NIBBLING OR CRUSHING
Birds aren't the only animals with beaks. Once an octopus or squid captures a meal with its many arms, it directs the food to its parrotlike beak. It then crushes its food and starts nibbling.

SCOOPING
Unlike other bird beaks, a pelican's beak isn't completely hard. The beak has an expandable pouch that can hold up to three gallons (11 L) of water as the bird scoops up fish.

Sharks have some nasty-looking teeth, and if you look closely, you'll notice they come in many shapes and sizes, with each type having a slightly different use.

TEARING

White sharks, commonly known as great whites, have serrated teeth for tearing chunks of flesh from large prey, such as seals and dolphins.

WHAT'S THE POINT?

Not all sharks have a use for their teeth. Large whale sharks and basking sharks are filter feeders. They use the bristles on their gills to separate tiny shrimplike zooplankton from ocean water. They then swallow their prey whole—no teeth necessary.

GRASPING

Sharks such as sand sharks have long, pointed teeth that curve backward for holding on to slippery, struggling fish.

The North American brown bear, often called a grizzly bear, is an excellent fisher.

SWIPE, CHOMP, SWALLOW

2

SKILLS AND TRICKS

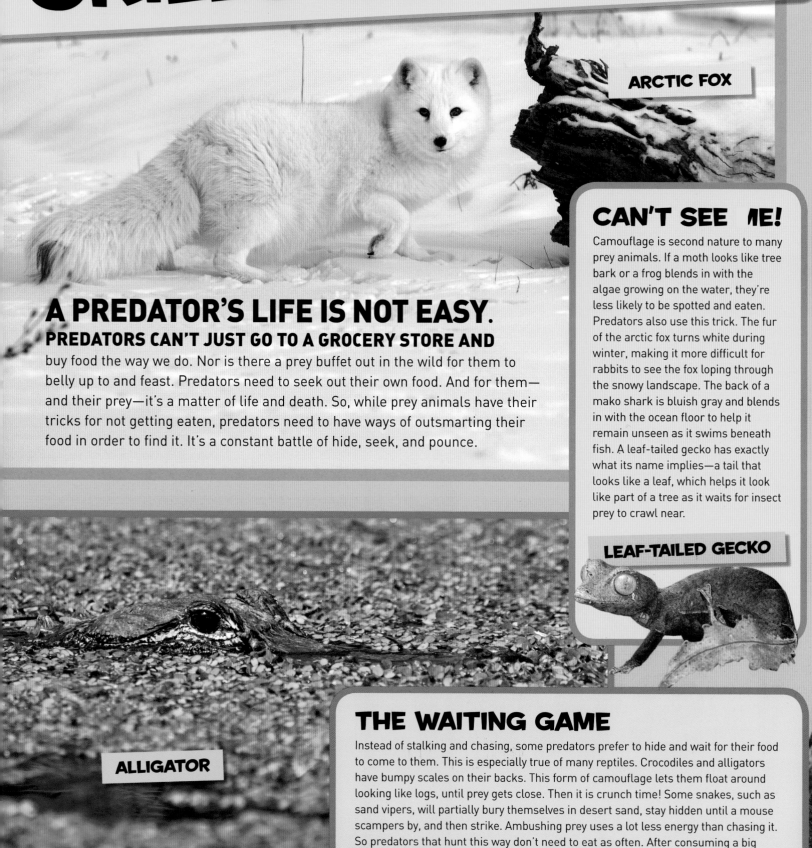

ARCTIC FOX

A PREDATOR'S LIFE IS NOT EASY.
PREDATORS CAN'T JUST GO TO A GROCERY STORE AND
buy food the way we do. Nor is there a prey buffet out in the wild for them to belly up to and feast. Predators need to seek out their own food. And for them—and their prey—it's a matter of life and death. So, while prey animals have their tricks for not getting eaten, predators need to have ways of outsmarting their food in order to find it. It's a constant battle of hide, seek, and pounce.

CAN'T SEE ME!
Camouflage is second nature to many prey animals. If a moth looks like tree bark or a frog blends in with the algae growing on the water, they're less likely to be spotted and eaten. Predators also use this trick. The fur of the arctic fox turns white during winter, making it more difficult for rabbits to see the fox loping through the snowy landscape. The back of a mako shark is bluish gray and blends in with the ocean floor to help it remain unseen as it swims beneath fish. A leaf-tailed gecko has exactly what its name implies—a tail that looks like a leaf, which helps it look like part of a tree as it waits for insect prey to crawl near.

LEAF-TAILED GECKO

ALLIGATOR

THE WAITING GAME
Instead of stalking and chasing, some predators prefer to hide and wait for their food to come to them. This is especially true of many reptiles. Crocodiles and alligators have bumpy scales on their backs. This form of camouflage lets them float around looking like logs, until prey gets close. Then it is crunch time! Some snakes, such as sand vipers, will partially bury themselves in desert sand, stay hidden until a mouse scampers by, and then strike. Ambushing prey uses a lot less energy than chasing it. So predators that hunt this way don't need to eat as often. After consuming a big meal, some reptiles can go days, weeks, or even months without eating.

TRAPDOOR SPIDER

TRAPS AND TRICKERY

Spiderwebs are spectacular feats of construction, but they're basically food traps. Insects and other small animals get stuck in their sticky strands, then the spider moves in for the kill. Not all spiders spin webs to capture their prey, however. A trapdoor spider will dig a burrow and add a trapdoor made of its own silk, as well as dirt and vegetation. Then it waits in the burrow until a tasty morsel walks by. The trapdoor springs open, and the spider drags its surprised victim into its den for lunch.

A margay is a small wild cat that lives in the trees of South American rain forests. Scientists believe it can make noises that sound somewhat like a monkey. When a real monkey comes to investigate, the margay pounces.

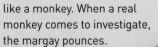
MARGAY

THERE YOU ARE!

While prey animals have their tricks for staying hidden, predators have special ways of sensing their next meal.

ECHOLOCATION

Bats use sonar to locate prey. They emit a high-pitched call, then listen for the sound waves bouncing off a bug. This helps them pinpoint the bug's location.

DEPTH PERCEPTION

PUMA

Many predators have their eyes located on the front of their head. This gives them a narrow, straightforward field of vision. But their eye position lets them know how close or far away things are. Depth perception is what helps a puma know how far to jump before it pounces on its prey.

HEARING

Some owls have one ear positioned higher on their head than the other. This helps them pinpoint where a sound is coming from. It's what allows a barn owl to swoop down on a mouse without being able to see it.

BARN OWL

TOUCH

CHEETAH

Whiskers aren't just adornments on a cat's face. They aid in hunting, especially at night. Animals that stalk prey at night can feel their surroundings as their whiskers brush up against things. They can feel out prey to catch and obstacles to avoid.

SMELL

The world is full of odors that we can't smell. But many predators, such as snakes, use their sense of smell to locate prey. When snakes flick out their tongues, they're actually picking up scent particles to help them know if food is near.

BURMESE PYTHON

FACT BITE: SEAHORSES ARE PREDATORS THAT USE THEIR SNOUTS TO SUCK IN AND EAT CRUSTACEANS.

SO STEALTHY!

ONCE PREY IS SPOTTED, THE NEXT CHALLENGE BEGINS.

PREDATORS HAVE TO CATCH THEIR FOOD. THERE ARE MANY WAYS THEY CAN DO THIS. THEY

can make a quick strike or a surprise attack. Some predators may form groups or use their own brute strength to overwhelm their prey. Others use speed and cunning. Still, predators fail more often than they succeed. For example, lions hunting alone are successful in only about one out of six hunts.

CHEETAH

STALKING AND POUNCING

Mammals are warm-blooded, and maintaining their body temperature uses a lot of energy. Most mammals hunt for food daily. But, to hunt successfully, they need a plan of attack. Wild cats such as bobcats, cougars, lynx, or mountain lions are known for stalking prey. With their padded paws, they can quietly sneak up on animals. Then, when they are close enough, they pounce. Bobcats may lurk in trees, whereas other wild felines, such as cheetahs, hide in tall grasses. The key is to get as close as possible, then use a quick burst of speed to catch the prey unaware.

STRENGTH IN NUMBERS

Sometimes a team effort is needed. This is frequently true of animals such as wolves, lions, dolphins, and hyenas. Insects working together can have devastating effects. A colony of army ants can overpower much larger insects and birds with their massive numbers. Some hornets, such as large Japanese giant hornets, will also team up to tackle their prey. A few dozen of these thumb-size giants can take out a hive with tens of thousands of smaller bees. Then the Japanese giant hornets bring the bodies of the bees back to their hive to feed their young.

JAPANESE GIANT HORNET

FACT BITE: A POLAR BEAR CAN KILL A SEAL WITH JUST ONE SWIPE OF ITS POWERFUL, CLAWED PAW.

BRUTE STRENGTH

Speed leads to some of the most dramatic chases in the animal world, but there are also epic battles of strength. Boas and pythons rely on their incredibly muscular bodies to subdue their prey. Once one of these constrictors gets hold of an animal, it wraps its body around the prey and slowly squeezes it to death. The amazing thing is that some snakes, such as anacondas, are strong enough to tackle large animals, including caimans, which are top predators themselves. Battles between these bruisers can take hours.

An African rock python wraps around and squeezes a Nile crocodile.

BOMBS AWAY!

Peregrine falcons are the fastest animals on Earth, and like other birds of prey, they have excellent eyesight. So they can fly high overhead, where their prey does not see them. Just the impact of their slamming into their prey can stun or kill the animal.

PEREGRINE FALCON

A GIANT MOUTHFUL

Amazingly, some of the largest animals on the planet eat some of the smallest. Whale sharks and basking sharks are filter feeders. They swim through the ocean with their mouths open, sucking up water and tiny shrimplike animals called zooplankton. Then they close their mouth, like a giant trap, and squeeze the water out through their gills. Bristles on their gills separate their food from the water, keeping the zooplankton in. Some whales are also filter feeders. They're called baleen whales. Instead of teeth, they have baleen which keeps their food in while letting the water out.

BALEEN WHALE

HOW PREY AVOID PREDATORS

THEY USE CAMOUFLAGE.

Animals use camouflage to look like something they are not, such as a green katydid looking like a leaf.

THEY ZIGZAG.

Rabbits will zigzag as they run from danger to make it more difficult to follow them.

THEY OUTLAST PREDATORS.

While a cheetah can outpace a gazelle over a short distance, the gazelle can outlast the cheetah if the race lasts more than a few seconds.

THEY HEAD FOR THE TREES!

Prey animals tend to be smaller and lighter than their predators, so a small monkey is safe from a heavy python way up in the treetops.

THEY HEAD UNDERGROUND.

Animals that live in burrows usually travel through tunnels that they dig to suit their size. This slows down larger predators that cannot fit in the tunnels to follow their prey.

THEY PLAY DEAD.

Animals such as opossums will play dead to trick predators, especially those predators that like eating a fresh kill.

THEY PUMP UP.

The rule of thumb is that usually predators are larger than their prey. However, some animals, such as pufferfish, can appear larger than life when they need to, so they look like more than a mouthful.

THEY POST LOOKOUTS.

Meerkats live in communities called mobs, and while some are snacking on insects or playing around, others are on the lookout for danger. A couple of chirps will send the whole mob underground to their burrows.

CLAWS AND TALONS

MANY PREDATORS HAVE

CLAWS, TALONS, OR PINCERS. THESE ACT as weapons that make grasping, killing, and eating quick and efficient. Each serves a purpose, and each predator uses its natural weaponry in different ways.

BONE-CRUSHING TALONS

Talons are fingerlike claws found on birds of prey. Hawk talons can be up to two inches (5 cm) long. Not only are their talons sharp, but birds of prey have powerful grips, too. Scientists believe their grip is at least ten times stronger than ours. It can be literally bone crushing. So once a hawk snatches a rabbit or snake, the victim is likely to get away.

EXPLORER'S CORNER

Some predators bring down their prey, and then climb trees where they can stash their food so other predators don't come and steal it. Many people think that leopards are the only predator that climbs trees, but lions also climb trees! In Samburu, we often see cubs climbing trees and playing in them. One day I saw our big male lion, Loirish, climb a sausage tree! But he got stuck at the top and had a hard time coming down.

DIG ME A HOLE

Dogs can be great diggers, no question. But a badger will outdig a dog any day. Badgers may not be as big as most dogs, but they have longer claws and powerful limbs. It takes a badger about a minute to dig a hole big enough for it to fit into. That skill comes in handy, especially when hunting prairie dogs or rabbits that dwell underground. Badgers will sniff out their prey's whereabouts, then start digging.

PINCER GRIP

Sometimes it's not about killing prey, it's just about holding on to it. Crabs and scorpions don't have claws or talons. Instead, they have viselike pincers. They use these pincers to snag and hold on to prey. Then once they have their prey under control, they can bring it to their mouth for a quick nibble.

THE MANY USES OF CLAWS

If you've ever watched your pet cat (or dog) scratch itself, you'll see how claws are useful. But how do some other predators use their claws?

- **FOR CLIMBING, OR CHASING PREY UP A TREE**
- **FOR GRASPING, OR HOLDING ON TO PREY**
- **FOR DEFENDING, OR FIGHTING OFF LARGER PREDATORS FOR FOOD**
- **FOR RAKING, OR DRAGGING ACROSS A PREY'S BODY TO MAIM IT**
- **FOR PUNCHING, OR DELIVERING A KNOCKOUT BLOW TO PREY**

CLIMBING

GRASPING

FACT BITES: ALL CATS, EXCEPT FOR CHEETAHS, HAVE RETRACTABLE CLAWS.

CHAMPION CHOMPERS

WHEN YOU THINK OF SHARKS AND SNAKES,
DO YOU THINK OF TEETH AND FANGS? THAT'S PROBABLY BECAUSE
they help make these predators deadly. Unlike people, who use their teeth mostly for chewing food, predators also rely on the power of their jaws and the sharpness of their teeth to catch and kill prey. The list of predators with killer teeth may include some surprises.

SNAKE TEETH

Snake teeth come in two varieties. Venomous snakes have fangs, hollow or grooved, that deliver venom to their prey. Constrictors have inwardly curved teeth designed to hold on to their prey as they squeeze it to death.

BUSH VIPER

This bush viper's fangs are drawn back into its sheaths.

MY, WHAT A BIG TOOTH YOU HAVE!

Narwhals possibly inspired stories of unicorns. But what we once thought were long, pointy horns are actually teeth, or tusks, that can grow nearly ten feet (3 m) long. But, they don't aid the narwhal in catching prey or eating.

FACT BITES: DESPITE THEIR NASTY TEETH, SOME PIRANHAS ARE PLANT-EATERS.

STAG BEETLE

MUNCHING WITH MANDIBLES

On some insects, mandibles look almost like a pair of serrated scissors. These are used for dicing prey up into edible bites. The mandibles of some beetles allow them to bite flesh and to suck fluids such as blood.

BULLDOG ANT

CONE SNAIL

Narwhals are porpoises that live in the Arctic Ocean. The spiral tusk of the male narwhal grows through its upper lip.

FLESH-EATING SNAIL

Snails may not seem like predators, but some, such as cone snails, are meat-eaters. These snails have a spearlike tooth they use to stab their prey and to inject venom. They eat fish, mollusks, worms, and other snails. Some scientists believe that snail teeth are one of the strongest natural substances on Earth. They aren't quite like our teeth, though, as they are microscopic in size and made of minerals.

NARWHAL

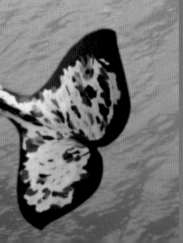

A PHOTO GALLERY

WITH SO MANY PREDATORS OUT THERE IN

the world, it's hard to pick the most effective. For some, it's their sheer size that makes them top predators, whereas for others, it's their fierce bite.

FEARSOME FLESH-EATERS

The cassowary, a large, odd-looking flightless bird from Australia and New Guinea, is not to be messed with. An omnivore, it will eat snails and frogs, as well as fruit. It is known for its powerful kick and sharp claws used to defend itself.

Spiders can be scary no matter their size, but when they grow to the size of your hand and eat birds, that's just terrifying—but also a little cool. The Goliath bird-eating spider also has one-inch (3-cm)-long fangs. This fierce and mighty arachnid is native to South America.

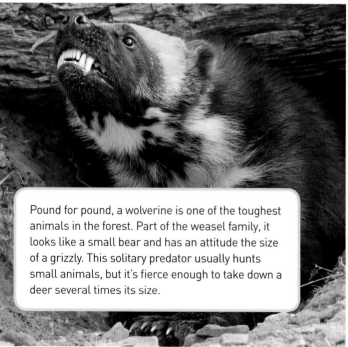

Pound for pound, a wolverine is one of the toughest animals in the forest. Part of the weasel family, it looks like a small bear and has an attitude the size of a grizzly. This solitary predator usually hunts small animals, but it's fierce enough to take down a deer several times its size.

Orcas, also called killer whales, have long, sharp teeth for eating tough prey such as sea lions and seals. These large dolphins are also known for preying on whales.

With a bite force of 3,700 pounds per square inch, the saltwater crocodile is one of the world's most dangerous predators. An adult fears nothing and can tackle a water buffalo or wild boar.

A Komodo dragon is machinelike in its pursuit of prey. Once this Indonesian predator bites an animal, it and all of its friends will follow the scent of blood from the wound. No matter how far away the animal gets or how fast it is, it won't get away, because the dragon's venom will ultimately weaken and kill it.

3

PREDATORS EVERYWHERE

An orca sneaks up on a group of seals near the ocean shore. Orcas are found in every ocean.

PREHISTORIC PREDATORS

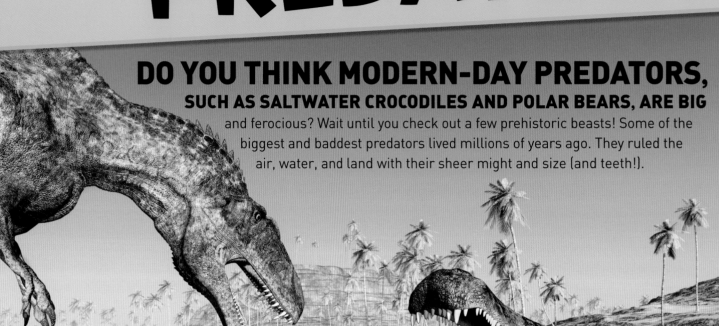

DO YOU THINK MODERN-DAY PREDATORS,
SUCH AS SALTWATER CROCODILES AND POLAR BEARS, ARE BIG

and ferocious? Wait until you check out a few prehistoric beasts! Some of the biggest and baddest predators lived millions of years ago. They ruled the air, water, and land with their sheer might and size (and teeth!).

SUPER CROC

Crocodiles are the largest reptiles living today, measuring up to 20 feet (6 m) long and weighing half a ton (454 kg). But reptiles were supersize in prehistoric times. *Sarcosuchus*, a crocodile-like beast nicknamed Super Croc, lived approximately 110 million years ago. It grew up to 40 feet (12 m) long and had foot-long (30-cm) teeth. Although it ate mostly fish, it could also make lunch out of small dinosaurs.

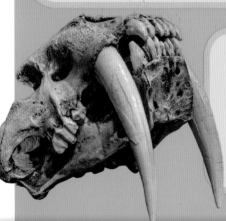

SUPER CAT

It seems like everything back in prehistoric times was supersize. That's true of the saber-toothed cat's teeth, as well—if "saber" wasn't enough of a clue. This giant cat had canine teeth that grew up to seven inches (18 cm) long. That's more than twice what the biggest cats sport nowadays. Its teeth were perfect for slicing and ripping flesh from its prehistoric prey, such as horses.

FACT BITE: PTEROSAURS COULD FLY, BUT THESE REPTILES ARE NOT RELATED TO BIRDS.

RULER OF THE LAND

One of the most feared predators among dinosaurs was the *Tyrannosaurus rex*. This mighty beast is among the largest carnivores to have lived on the planet. It most likely killed by taking big bites out of its prey with its huge, bone-crunching jaws, which came armed with eight-inch (20-cm) teeth.

ICHTHYOSAUR

T. REX

RULER OF THE SEAS

During prehistoric times, the world's oceans were filled with dangerous creatures—mostly animals with sharp teeth and ravenous appetites. Among them was the ichthyosaur, growing up to 30 feet (9 m) long. It was a strong swimmer, snacking on fish, octopuses, and just about anything else that couldn't outswim it.

SHORT-FACED BEAR

This beast lived about 11,000 years ago and would make today's grizzlies look small. It stood more than ten feet (3 m) tall and weighed up to a ton (1 t). The short-faced bear is also nicknamed the "running bear," as it had long legs and could possibly reach speeds of 40 miles an hour (64 km/h) while chasing down deer and bison.

SHORT-FACED BEAR

RULER OF THE AIR

PTEROSAUR

While *T. rex* ruled the land in prehistoric times, the pterosaurs ruled the air. With a wingspan of up to 40 feet (12 m), this winged dinosaur was bigger than a jet fighter. It swooped down to catch fresh fish but was also a scavenger.

LAND PREDATORS

IS THAT A PREDATOR IN YOUR
LIVING ROOM? WHAT ABOUT OUTSIDE YOUR HOME?

Land predators can be wild and majestic, like lions and bears. But you may also be living with a top predator: your pet cat!

CHIMPANZEE

ARMED AND READY

Primates are among the smartest animals on Earth. And with intelligence comes the ability to use tools. Scientists have witnessed chimpanzees using twigs to fish termites out of their nests. Of course, we've topped that. Humans may not be the fastest or strongest of land predators, but we are smart. And we've developed many tools for getting food—from fishing rods to rifles and traps.

FLUFFY AND FIDO

Some of the most dangerous land predators live among us. House cats, like their larger cousins, are expert hunters. It's estimated that they kill millions of songbirds each year. So keep that in mind when deciding to let Tiger roam around your backyard. Dogs, when given a chance, will form packs just as their wolf relatives do. And many have what's called a prey drive, an instinct to chase rabbits, squirrels, or any other furry creature that runs in front of them. Sometimes packs of dogs chase down deer, and they've been known to attack farm animals.

EXPLORER'S CORNER

Lions hunt frequently. I have watched lions kill animals ranging in size from a warthog to a giraffe! Lions also scavenge, and they will feed on animals that have died in other ways. I once watched an elephant die of natural causes and a whole pride of lions fed on her for more than a week. They were all over the carcass—even inside the stomach!

Here's the answer to the question I posed on page 7: I was taking photos of African wild dogs, also known as hunting dogs or painted dogs. They are considered an endangered predator.

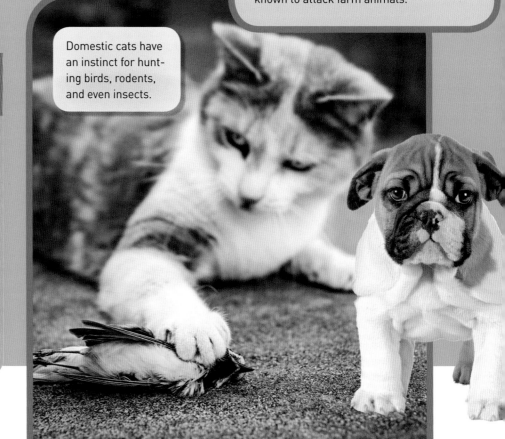

Domestic cats have an instinct for hunting birds, rodents, and even insects.

STICKY TONGUES

Not all animals stalk their prey. Some, such as salamanders and frogs, just need their food to get within tongue range. Then they shoot out their tongue like a sticky-tipped missile and snatch their meals.

POWER SNIFFERS

Sometimes a strong sense of smell works better than excellent eyesight, especially when prey is camouflaged, or when it is far away. The nose is not so easily fooled. Predators often smell their prey before actually seeing it, which also means they likely haven't been seen. That gives them an opportunity to sneak in close before pouncing. Wolves and dogs have great smelling ability, but bears are the best sniffers. Their big noses have thousands of smell receptors.

RATTLE ME

Not all animals have senses that work quite like ours. Snakes, for example, don't have ear openings to catch sound waves. But that doesn't mean they're deaf. Instead, sound waves rattle their skulls, and the snakes translate those vibrations into sound. They can also detect vibrations in the ground. That helps them know if danger is approaching or if food is getting close.

FOREST VIPER

FACT BITE: LADYBUGS ARE PREDATORS. THEY EAT APHIDS.

MARINE PREDATORS

WATER COVERS MORE THAN
70 PERCENT OF EARTH'S SURFACE. STRETCHES

of ocean that reach miles deep into total darkness make for an incredibly large and diverse habitat for creatures of all kinds. The oceans are so expansive that they might as well be another planet, and we have yet to explore all their depths or discover all their secrets. Within these vast depths are some of the deadliest and most interesting predators of all.

JELLYFISH

DON'T TOUCH THAT

Jellyfish are some of the world's most beautiful creatures. They are also some of the deadliest. The tentacles trailing behind their umbrella-shaped bodies are covered in stinging cells. If a fish, crab, or shrimp gets stung, it will be stunned or paralyzed, then pulled into the jellyfish's body to be digested. Jellyfish don't prey on people, but people do accidently get stung sometimes. The stings are painful, and some, such as those of the box jellyfish, can be deadly.

ANGLERFISH

IF LOOKS COULD KILL

Little, if any, light illuminates the deepest reaches of the world's oceans. That's probably a good thing, as some of the creepiest-looking critters live there—from viperfish to saber-tooth fish. While small, at less than one foot (30 cm) long, these fish are fierce looking. In a world in which predators cannot see to hunt their prey, some have developed a clever way for food to come to them. Anglerfish have a growth that extends from their head. The end glows and acts as a lure, attracting shrimp and small fish.

FACT BITE: STINGRAYS USE THE BARBED STINGER ON THEIR TAIL FOR DEFENSE.

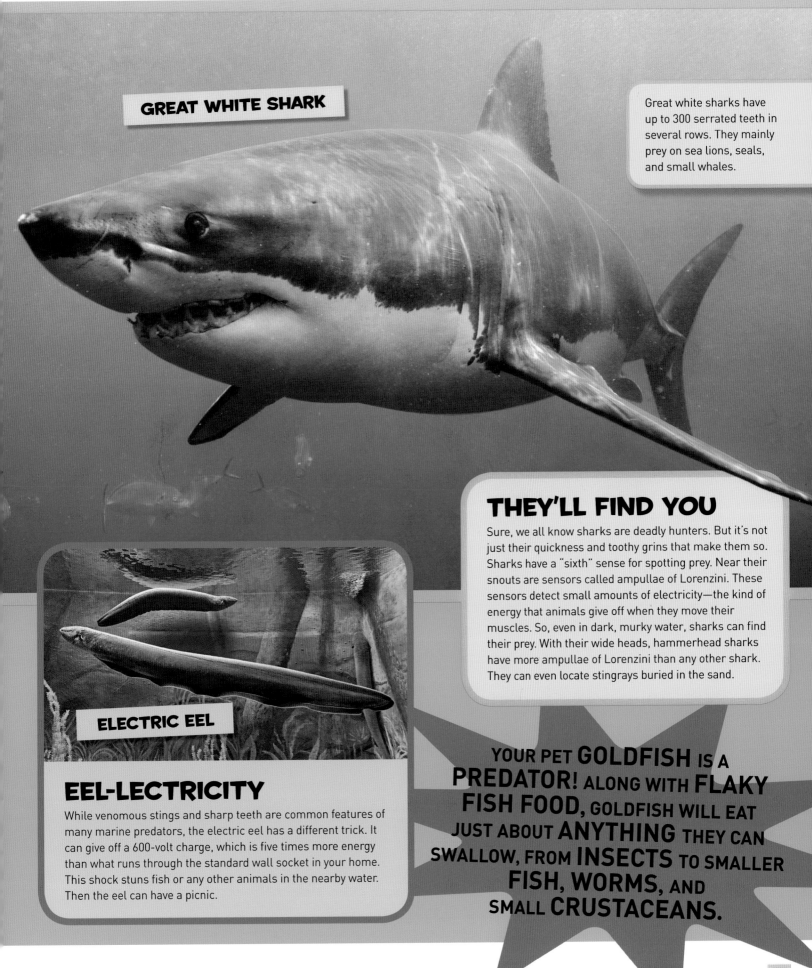

GREAT WHITE SHARK

Great white sharks have up to 300 serrated teeth in several rows. They mainly prey on sea lions, seals, and small whales.

THEY'LL FIND YOU

Sure, we all know sharks are deadly hunters. But it's not just their quickness and toothy grins that make them so. Sharks have a "sixth" sense for spotting prey. Near their snouts are sensors called ampullae of Lorenzini. These sensors detect small amounts of electricity—the kind of energy that animals give off when they move their muscles. So, even in dark, murky water, sharks can find their prey. With their wide heads, hammerhead sharks have more ampullae of Lorenzini than any other shark. They can even locate stingrays buried in the sand.

ELECTRIC EEL

EEL-LECTRICITY

While venomous stings and sharp teeth are common features of many marine predators, the electric eel has a different trick. It can give off a 600-volt charge, which is five times more energy than what runs through the standard wall socket in your home. This shock stuns fish or any other animals in the nearby water. Then the eel can have a picnic.

YOUR PET **GOLDFISH** IS A **PREDATOR!** ALONG WITH **FLAKY FISH FOOD,** GOLDFISH WILL EAT JUST ABOUT **ANYTHING** THEY CAN SWALLOW, FROM **INSECTS** TO SMALLER **FISH, WORMS,** AND SMALL **CRUSTACEANS.**

FLYING PREDATORS

BIRDS MAY RULE THE SKIES, BUT THEY AREN'T
THE ONLY PREDATORS FLYING THROUGH THE AIR. INSECTS, FROM DRAGONFLIES

to beetles, wasps, and flies have wings, too, and they also need to eat. Here are just some of the amazing number of predators buzzing around our heads.

DRAGONFLY

PHILIPPINE EAGLE

DEADLY DRAGONFLIES

We mostly think of flying insects as pests, such as flies. Dragonflies are helpful insects because they eat other insect pests such as mosquitoes that carry diseases. They are also ace pilots when it comes to buzzing around. They can fly in just about any direction and even hover, which allows them to snatch pests in midair.

MONKEY-EATER

The Philippine eagle is a monkey-eater. This powerful bird is among the largest and strongest birds of prey. Pairs of them will sometimes work together to hunt. One will perch in a branch to distract the monkeys, while the other swoops down from above. Lemurs and monitor lizards also make up part of this predator's diet.

FACT BITE: BATS ARE NOT "BLIND," AND MANY SEE AS WELL AS HUMANS.

MY, WHAT BIG EARS YOU HAVE!

If you've ever been brave enough to look closely at a bat, you will have noticed that they have huge ears on their small heads. Their ears work like radar, catching sound waves the bats have emitted. The sound waves bounce off their prey, flying insects, pinpointing their location. And be thankful for these fluffy fliers. One bat can eat hundreds of mosquitos in one night.

BACKYARD PREDATORS

Look in your backyard or scan your neighborhood park. Predators live everywhere. You may have snakes or lizards hiding in a nearby woodpile, eating mice and bugs. But the most common predators are probably the flying ones. Songbirds tweet and chirp beautifully, but they also eat a lot of insects, keeping the population under control.

EASTERN BLUEBIRD

The birds in our backyards eat insects and invertebrates, as well as fruits, nuts, and seeds.

The Philippine eagle has a wingspan of up to 7 feet (2.1 m) and can weigh 14 pounds (6.4 kg).

41

PREDATOR COMPARISONS

YOU vs. ANIMAL PREDATORS

IF YOU HAVEN'T ALREADY FOUND THE predators in this book awe-inspiring and fearsome, let's check out how you would stack up against them. These comparisons may change your mind.

LACE UP YOUR RUNNING SHOES!

Many predators sneak up on their prey and then rely on a quick burst of speed to catch the animals off guard. Cheetahs are the speedsters among land animals. If you are fast, you can probably run a 100-meter dash in about 20 seconds. A cheetah can do that in less than 4 seconds.

MIGHTIEST OF THE MIGHTY

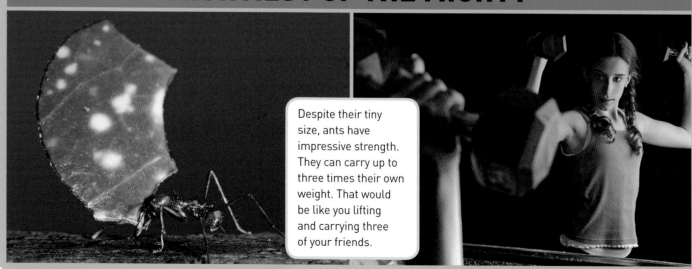

Despite their tiny size, ants have impressive strength. They can carry up to three times their own weight. That would be like you lifting and carrying three of your friends.

A TOOTHY SMILE

Felids, or wild cats, are known for their canines—the two pairs of long, pointy teeth toward the front of their mouth. In big cats such as tigers, these teeth can grow to nearly three inches (8 cm) in length, not counting the roots. Humans have canines, too. They are the slightly pointy teeth just in front of our molars, but our canines are hardly noticeable at about a half inch in length (1 cm).

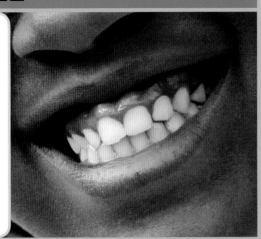

HUG YOUR FOOD

Constrictor snakes, such as boas and pythons, literally hug their food to death. They wrap their muscular body around their prey and squeeeeeeeze, stopping blood flow to their victim's heart. Could you imagine if you had to do that every time you ate a meal?

STICK OUT YOUR TONGUE

Chameleons are sharpshooters with their tongues. They use them to pick unsuspecting bugs off tree branches. Their tongues can be longer than their bodies. That would be the same as you sticking your tongue out far enough to touch the ground.

PREDATOR CHALLENGE

Vultures, like this king vulture from Central and South America, are mostly carrion-eaters. They eat everything from small dead lizards to dead cattle.

45

PREDATORS IN CULTURE

FACE IT, PREDATORS ARE IMPRESSIVE.
WHETHER IT'S BECAUSE OF THEIR LIGHTNING SPEED, BONE-CRUNCHING
jaws, or majestic looks, we find them fascinating subjects for stories, fables, and cartoons.

MATCH THE PICTURE TO THE STAR!

Some predators have become famous in books and movies. Can you match the animal to their fictional portrayal?

1 THIS HONEY-LOVER WAS CREATED BY AUTHOR A. A. MILNE.

2 THIS WISE ANIMAL IS MORE THAN 100 YEARS OLD AND ORIGINALLY APPEARS IN A BOOK BY RUDYARD KIPLING.

3 SON OF A GREAT KING, THIS PREDATOR RUNS AWAY FROM HIS PAST.

4 THIS LOVABLE PREDATOR WISHES HE HAD COURAGE.

5 HIS FAMILY IS KNOWN FOR ITS RUTHLESSNESS, BUT THIS GUY REFUSES TO BE A KILLER.

A

The Cowardly Lion helps Dorothy find the Emerald City in *The Wizard of Oz* (1939), originally a book by L. Frank Baum.

THE COWARDLY LION

KAA

B Kaa is an Indian rock python from *The Jungle Book*.

FACT BITE: "RIKKI-TIKKI-TAVI" IS A STORY FROM *THE JUNGLE BOOK* ABOUT A MONGOOSE SAVING A FAMILY FROM A NEST OF COBRAS.

ANSWERS: 1. C; 2. B; 3. E; 4. A; 5. D

WINNIE THE POOH

The bear called Winnie the Pooh has appeared in many books and films.

LENNY

Lenny is a shark trying to be a vegetarian in the animated movie *Shark Tale* (2004).

SIMBA

Simba, a young lion, struggles to replace his father as leader of the pride in *The Lion King* movie and musical.

PREDATOR PORTRAYALS

SCARY SHARK MOVIE

No movies gave people a fear of going in the water more than *Jaws* (1975) and its sequels. This series of movies portrayed great white sharks as large and aggressive killing machines. Don't believe it! Great white sharks can grow up to 20 feet (6 m) long and be deadly to their prey, but don't worry—humans aren't on the menu. Shark attacks usually occur only because of mistaken identity. Fewer than 100 shark attacks are confirmed each year, and, of those, only a handful are fatal.

KRAKEN OR GIANT SQUID?

Some of the most feared predators have appeared in myths and stories throughout the ages. Take the kraken, for instance. In Greek mythology, hero Perseus saves a woman from a kraken, a many-tentacled sea monster. In Jules Verne's novel *20,000 Leagues Under the Sea,* Captain Nemo's ship, the *Nautilus,* is attacked by an incredibly large squid. Where did ideas for this mythical monster come from? In all likelihood, way back when, someone saw a giant squid when a dead one washed up on shore. Giant squids can reach up to 30 feet (9 m) long.

BEEP-BEEP, POOR COYOTE

The fondness generations of humans have for the cartoon predator Wile E. Coyote isn't from a love of coyotes. It's because of his hapless attempts to catch the Road Runner, a speedster of a bird. We laugh at Wile E. Coyote's misadventures. But unlike the great white or giant squid discussed here, this coyote has been made out to be *less* frightening than he actually would be. In reality, coyotes are cunning and opportunistic predators. They'll go after cats, dogs, and small farm animals. And they are fast, too—a road runner would be no match.

FANGS, BEAKS, OR VENOM?

PREDATORS GET THEIR FOOD
IN SOME INCREDIBLE WAYS. HAVE YOU EVER
imagined that you had their skills and abilities? Take the quiz below to see your predator match.

WHAT'S YOUR PREDATOR PROFILE?

1 **What are your dining habits?**

A. You prefer to eat alone at a seaside bistro.

B. You sometimes like to eat out and share a meal with your pals.

C. Scrounging is your thing. You never turn down a free meal.

D. You'll often order a large meat-lovers' pizza for delivery and eat it all in one sitting.

2 **How would your friends describe you?**

A. You love your family, but sometimes like to be on your own.

B. Alone or in a pack, you can figure out how to deal.

C. You like hanging with a crowd for most things.

D. If no one bothers you when you are sunning or chilling, things will be fine.

3 **Your idea of a perfect vacation would be:**

A. By the water, but preferably in winter so you can go ice-skating or snowshoeing.

B. Camping in a forest or somewhere with lots of nature.

C. Anywhere you can soar and fly.

D. Soaking up some rays in the summer, or huddled under a warm blanket in the winter.

4 **How would you describe your temper?**

A. Ferocious—you will get in the face of anyone who bugs you.

B. You will bare your teeth to protect yourself but would prefer to avoid confrontation.

C. Temper? What's that? You're so chill.

D. You'll give people plenty of warning before you strike.

5 **What is your clothing style?**

A. White. All white, whatever the season.

B. You prefer dark neutrals, such as gray, beige, and brown.

C. Sleek and black, all the way!

D. You are a fan of casual camouflage.

IF YOU SCORED MOSTLY A:
Look for you in a room and you'll be blending in with the white painted walls. Much like the polar bear, you are not a particularly social animal, but you will stay close to family. People know not to provoke you or overstep their bounds.

IF YOU SCORED MOSTLY B:
Like the gray wolf, you love your friends but also need some alone time so you don't start snarling and snapping at people. You have no problem bellying up to a buffet table with a pack of pals, but they better not steal that last chicken wing!

IF YOU SCORED MOSTLY C:
Hello, turkey vulture! You are a clever bird, with a special ability to take things as they come. You are always on the lookout for a free meal, and your pals enjoy tagging along when you find one.

IF YOU SCORED MOSTLY D:
Like a rattlesnake, you enjoy a solo hearty meal. You also prefer to blend in with your surroundings, and you don't go looking for trouble. But if trouble finds you, it will heed your warning to leave, or risk your venomous bite.

FACT BITE: RATTLESNAKES GIVE BIRTH TO LIVE YOUNG.

FACT VS. MYTH

OVER THE YEARS, MANY MYTHS HAVE BEEN TOLD ABOUT PREDATORS.

Often they are far-fetched stories told by someone who saw one of these mighty beasts up close and lived to tell about it. Such encounters can be on the scary side, and fear often leads to exaggeration. People have an instinct to jazz up their stories to make them more exciting for listeners. But still, even the most far-fetched tales often have a hint of truth to them. Can you tell fact from myth?

A WOLVES HOWL AT THE MOON.

B LARGE BIRDS OF PREY CAN CARRY OFF SMALL CHILDREN.

C VENOM CAN BE USED AS MEDICINE.

D A COYWOLF IS PART WOLF AND PART COYOTE.

E YOU CAN ESCAPE FROM A BEAR BY CLIMBING A TREE.

A. MYTH

Wolves howl to communicate with each other. They are often saying things like "Here I am!" or "This is my pack's territory." There is no scientific evidence that wolves howl at the moon, especially since the moon isn't about to howl back.

B. MYTH

Birds have hollow bones so they are light enough to fly. Weight is a huge factor for them. Even the strongest of birds can lift only a few pounds into the air. So while harpy eagles can carry off small monkeys, most young humans are a bit too heavy for them.

C. FACT

Scientists use snake venom to create antivenin—a cure for a venomous snakebite. Scientists are also researching how spider, scorpion, insect, and snake venom can be used medicinally for such things as cancer treatments.

D. FACT

The eastern coyote, sometimes called the coywolf, is a hybrid of the western coyote and eastern red wolf. They are larger than coyotes and smaller than wolves. Coywolves hunt in packs in rural and forested areas of the northeastern United States and parts of southern Canada.

E. MYTH

With their short, curved claws and strong limbs, all bears, especially cubs and small adults, can climb trees. Even large grizzlies and polar bears can manage it if they can find a tree that supports their weight, and if they have a reason (such as chasing prey) to climb it. And if they can't get up the tree, they might just knock it over.

FACT BITE: CROCODILES HAVE TEAR GLANDS NEAR THEIR THROATS, SO THEIR CHEWING ACTION MAKES THEM SHED TEARS.

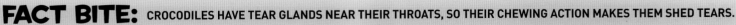

SURVIVAL SKILLS

YOU KNOW THAT PREDATORS HAVE SOME DEADLY ABILITIES. BUT THAT IS NOT A REASON TO FEAR THEM. KEEP YOUR DISTANCE AND

admire them from afar. Predators have the ability to survive and thrive in the natural world where every day is a life-or-death struggle. Almost all of us live in areas with potentially dangerous predators, from spiders to snakes, coyotes, and grizzly bears. Chance encounters will happen. But remember the saying "Don't poke the bear!" Just don't put yourself in a dangerous situation with a dangerous animal. In almost all cases, predators are not out to harm us, but that can change if an animal feels threatened. Here is some advice on how to play it safe with some common predators.

BEARS

Bears may look soft and cuddly, but don't try to hug them. Some bears, such as grizzlies, can be very territorial. Approaching them or even just looking at them may be viewed as a challenge. When it comes down to it, bear attacks occur mostly when people surprise or startle a bear. A scared bear is a dangerous bear. But if a bear hears you, it will avoid you. So when in bear country, be aware. Talk and make noise so the bears know you're there. And if you do see a bear, back away slowly. Only prey animals run.

GRIZZLY BEAR

FACT BITE: BLACK BEARS HAVE 42 TEETH.

SNAKES

If you live in an area with venomous snakes, learn what they look like. Being able to identify the snake that bit someone will help doctors treat the victim with the proper antivenin. Many snakes hide and lie in wait for prey, so sometimes you may accidently stumble across one no matter how careful you are. Luckily, snakes often give a warning before striking. It may be an angry hiss or rattling sound. Back away! If someone gets bitten, seek medical attention immediately.

BLACK WIDOW

ALLIGATORS AND CROCODILES

Alligators and crocodiles are among the most feared predators. They can grow to massive sizes and have bone-crunching bites. But as with all animals, playing it safe will keep you safe. If you share an area with these predators, avoid water except for designated swimming areas. This also means keeping pets away from ditches and ponds, because gators and crocs can end up in any body of water. Should you spy a gator or croc crawling out of the water toward you, don't zigzag as you run away (which is what some people say to do). Instead, follow the quickest escape route.

SPIDERS

These creepy crawlies are impossible to avoid. We love what they do (eat pesky bugs) but hate that they can get just about anywhere. The key is to know whether any potentially dangerous spiders, such as the brown recluse or black widow, live near you. The next step is to learn their habits. For example, these spiders will hide in woodpiles, so stack wood away from your house and use gloves when you do chores or when you poke around the woodpile.

Be aware when you live near predator habitat, and don't take chances.

AMERICAN ALLIGATOR

Here I am working with two warriors, to track a radio-collared lion. Collaring lions is important so we can follow their movements and see when they come close to villages.

LIONS ACROSS KENYA ARE IN DECLINE FOR TWO MAIN REASONS. THEY ARE

running out of space to live because their habitat has shrunk, and they are being killed. When lion habitat is encroached upon, or shared by humans for housing and livestock grazing land, lions really struggle to find enough food. The livestock, such as goats, sheep, and cattle, become easy meals. When lions kill livestock, the local people whose lives depend on that livestock are understandably very angry. Cattle are like money in a bank account for herders. They often go out and kill the lions to protect their livestock from future kills. This is why lions are disappearing so quickly from Kenya. In other parts of Africa, unsustainable hunting, the bushmeat trade (wild meat sold for people to eat), and trade in lion bones used as folk medicine are other reasons for the decline.

My team works to reverse the trends of dwindling predators through a number of education and awareness programs. We encourage people to live with lions. We talk to the local people about the importance of lions and conservation. We train them on better husbandry techniques and get them excited about being involved in conservation. Our aim is to make conservation a way of life in the communities that share land with lions. We work with warriors—young Samburu men, who are traditionally responsible for protecting their livestock from external threats such as predators. These warriors have become incredible ambassadors for wildlife. I also work with women whose knowledge has been very much neglected, but who now have a strong voice in conservation. What I like to do best is work with kids. My favorite moments have been working with young Kenyan children who may live close to National Parks but have never seen wildlife close-up. Through the work of the Ewaso Lions Project, many children have become wildlife leaders. They are the future of conservation. Showing them their first wild lion and seeing the smiles on their faces gives me hope for the future.

This lioness was injured badly after she entered a village at night and got stuck in a fence. We called a wildlife vet to help treat her. She was named Kofafeth, which means "strong lioness" in the local language. That's exactly what she is because she recovered within a few weeks.

AFTERWORD

PREDATORS ARE AN
IMPORTANT PART OF THE NATURAL WORLD.

Imagine if there were no wolves prowling the forests. Of course, the deer would like that—their main predator would be gone. But without wolves hunting them, deer herds would grow and grow. They would overpopulate their habitat and ravage their food supply. That would lead to starvation and many more deaths than the wolves would have caused. This is one reason why it is important to understand the importance of predators in our environments. Predators such as wolves and big cats tend to hunt the sickest, oldest, and weakest animals in a herd, because they are the easiest to catch. This is called culling. By culling the herds, predators actually help their prey by making sure only healthy animals mate and reproduce.

When checking the health of a natural area, scientists often look to the top predators. The number of predators in a habitat provides a clue to the environment's health. An area with several top predators has plenty of primary and secondary consumers to feed them. The plant life must be doing well there, too, because it is supporting the prey animals. If there are few predators, then odds are the area is in danger, whether from pollution; human encroachment on the animal habitat, such as building houses on lands where wild animals live; or other threats.

So, when you see a hawk circling overhead, or a snake slithering across your path, you can admire these predators for the deadly hunters they are. Remember that they kill only as a means to feed themselves and their young. Their presence is a sign that all is well in the natural world.

Wolves are the largest members of the dog family, and they live and hunt in packs. All of the wolves in a pack help take care of the pups.

A fox's thick tail helps it keep its balance and keep warm. Foxes are omnivores who will eat fruit and vegetables, as well as rodents, birds, fish, rabbits, and frogs.

Their powerful bite and serrated teeth give piranhas a reputation as fish to avoid. Researchers believe they are much like regular fish, but with razor teeth. Piranhas have been known to bite humans, but mostly when starving, or startled.

AN INTERACTIVE GLOSSARY

PREDATOR PROSE

A great white shark thrusts out of the ocean with a seal in its mouth.

THINK YOU'RE AN EXPERT ON PREDATORS?

Check out these words and test your knowledge! Read through these terms and meanings, and build your vocabulary. Then check out the page numbers to see them used in context. The answers are listed at the bottom of this page.

1. Birds of Prey

Birds with razor-sharp talons, hooked beaks, and keen eyesight, that feed on other animals. Also called raptors.
(PAGES 14, 15, 18, 25, 26, 40, 50)

Which of these birds are considered to be birds of prey?

a. owls

b. herons

c. pelicans

d. eagles

2. Camouflage

An animal's natural coloring or form that allows it to blend in with its environment or surroundings
(PAGES 22, 25, 37)

What are examples of predator camouflage?

a. a mako shark's bluish-gray back

b. the bumpy scales on an alligator's back

c. an arctic fox's snow-white fur

d. all of the above

3. Canids

A group of doglike animals
(PAGE 11)

Which animal is not a canid?

a. coyote

b. fox

c. wolf

d. wolverine

4. Carrion

The decaying flesh of dead animals
(PAGES 10, 11, 45)

Why would an animal eat carrion?

a. carrion does not fight back

b. it uses less energy than hunting

c. carrion is easier to find

d. all of the above

5. Carnivores

Animal that feed only on meat, or flesh
(PAGES 11, 13, 15, 35)

Which animal is a carnivore?

a. black bear

b. elephant

c. rat snake

d. vampire bat

6. Decomposers

Bacteria and fungi that feed on dead animals and plants and return nutrients into the soil
(PAGES 12, 13)

What don't decomposers do?

a. stalk and hunt prey

b. help plants grow by making soil rich

c. break down dead plants and animals

d. help ensure a healthy ecosystem

7. Felids

A group of catlike animals
(PAGE 43)

Which animals are not felids?

a. badger

b. ferret

c. lion

d. margay

8. Herbivores

Animals that eat only plants
(PAGE 13)

Which animal is a herbivore?

a. black bear

b. elephant

c. rat snake

d. vampire bat

9. Omnivores

Animals that eat both meat and plants
(PAGES 11, 13, 30, 57)

Which animal is not an omnivore?

a. lion

b. chimpanzee

c. bear

d. cockroach

10. Parasites

Animals that feed and live on a host animal
(PAGE 11)

What is an example of a parasite?

a. grasshopper

b. lice

c. mosquito

d. vampire bat

11. Scavengers

Animals that feed on carrion and/or dead plant matter
(PAGES 11, 35)

What kind of behaviors do scavengers display ?

a. some eat together in groups

b. they pick over the carcass of another animal's kill

c. they chase down prey

d. they eat decaying flesh

12. Venom

A poison that some animals inject into their prey to paralyze or kill it
(PAGES 15, 28, 29, 31, 48–49, 50–51, 52)

Venom is injected through?

a. spitting

b. biting or stinging

c. claws

d. squeezing

ANSWERS: **1.** a and d; **2.** d; **3.** d; **4.** d; **5.** c; **6.** a; **7.** a and b; **8.** b; **9.** a; **10.** b; **11.** a, b, and d; **12.** b

FIND OUT MORE

Feel like taking a bite out of more facts? Or what about clawing your way through more books? Try these resources for more information.

PREDATORS ON FILM

Kids: Ask your parents for permission to watch.

The Secret Life of Predators
National Geographic Channel, 2013

PLACES TO VISIT

American Museum of Natural History
Central Park West at 79th Street,
New York, NY 10024-5192
www.amnh.org

Australian Museum
1 William Street,
Sydney NSW 2010
www.australianmuseum.net.au

Natural History Museum, United Kingdom
Cromwell Road, London SW7 5BD
www.nhm.ac.uk

PRETTY SPECIAL PREDATOR READS

Everything Big Cats
by Elizabeth Carney
National Geographic Children's Books, 2011

Everything Birds of Prey
by Blake Hoena
National Geographic Children's Books, 2015

Everything Sharks
by Ruth Musgrave
National Geographic Children's Books, 2011

**Editorial, Design, and Production by
   Plan B Book Packagers**

Captions
Cover: The male lion is easily recognized by its wild mane.
Page 1: A wolverine bares its teeth.
Pages 2–3: Wolves chase prey through deep snow.

Since 1888, the National Geographic Society has funded more
than 12,000 research, exploration, and preservation projects
around the world. The Society receives funds from National
Geographic Partners LLC, funded in part by your purchase. A
portion of the proceeds from this book supports this vital work.
To learn more, visit www.natgeo.com/info.

For more information, visit www.nationalgeographic.com, call
1-800-647-5463, or write to the following address:
National Geographic Partners
1145 17th Street N.W.
Washington, D.C. 20036-4688 U.S.A.

Visit us online at nationalgeographic.com/books

For librarians and teachers: ngchildrensbooks.org

More for kids from National Geographic: kids.nationalgeo-
graphic.com

For information about special discounts for bulk purchases,
please contact National Geographic Books Special Sales:
ngspecsales@ngs.org

For rights or permissions inquiries, please contact National
Geographic Books Subsidiary Rights: ngbookrights@ngs.org

Paperback ISBN: 978-1-4263-2534-2
Reinforced library binding ISBN: 978-1-4263-2535-9

Printed in Hong Kong
16/THK/1